Young ELI Read

Edith Nesbit

Five Children and It

Retold and activities by Jane Cadwallader
Illustrated by Gustavo Mazali

Five children, Cyril, Anthea,
Robert, Jane and their baby brother,
the Lamb, lived in a big white house
in the countryside. The baby was called
the Lamb because the first thing he
said was 'Baaaa!'

At the time of our story the five children were at home with their nanny, Martha, and the cook. Father and Mother were away but the children were happy, playing and digging in the sand pit at the bottom of the garden.

3 One day the children were at the sandpit when suddenly Anthea said, 'Oh! Look! What a strange animal!' It had lots of fur, hands like a monkey and ears like a bat. But the strangest thing about it was its eyes. They were on long horns like a snail's. 'I beg your pardon! I'm *not* a strange animal! I'm a Sand Fairy and I can give you one wish every day.' The children looked at the Sand Fairy in surprise. 'Wow!' said Robert, 'A wish every day?' 'Yes,' said the Sand Fairy, 'but the wish goes away at sunset.'

▶ 4 Anthea said, 'We want to be as beautiful as the day and night!' The Sand Fairy's body began to get bigger and bigger and bigger. Then it said, 'You've got your wish,' and it disappeared into the sand.

The children looked at each
other. Their hair was as yellow
as the sun and their eyes as blue
as the sky. They were all very
beautiful! The Lamb began to
cry.

Lamb!
Don't cry!
It's only us!

5 The children went to the house for tea but Martha said, 'Who are you? Why have you got the Lamb? Poor baby! Give him to me and go away!' and she closed the door.

Tell *my* children it's time for tea.

8

The children were very hungry, but what could they do? They went to sit under a tree until the sun went down and the wish went away.

Oh good! You look like Anthea again!

The next day, the children ran down to the sand pit. The Sand Fairy was grumpy, but Cyril said, 'We've got a wish. We want pots of gold!' The Sand Fairy said 'Humph,' but its body got bigger and bigger and bigger. Then it said, 'You've got your wish,' and it disappeared into the sand.

The children looked at the pots of gold.
'Wow!' said Cyril, 'We can buy lots of
things!'

7 The children walked quickly to the shops... Well, as quickly as they could. Remember they had to push the Lamb's pushchair and carry the heavy pots of gold! On the way, they said what they wanted to buy. 'Some comics,' said Cyril. 'Ice creams,' said Robert. 'A sweater for the Lamb and a scarf for me,' said Anthea. 'A parrot,' said Jane.

They went to a shop
to buy ice creams.
But, oh dear!

8 Then they went to the bookshop, and the clothes shop and the pet shop… But everywhere the shopkeepers said the same.

Sorry. That money is no good.

Sorry. That money is no good.

Sorry. That money is no good.

The children were very hungry
and thirsty but what could they
do? They went to sit under a tree
until the sunset and the wish went
away. Then they walked slowly
back home.

The next day was cloudy and cold, but the
children put on their coats and boots and ran
down to the sand pit. On the way Robert said,
'I would love to live in a castle.'
When the children found the Sand Fairy it was
very grumpy! 'You woke me up!' it said. 'But
we've got a wish!' said Robert. 'You can only
have one wish a day,' said the Sand Fairy before
it disappeared into the sand.

The children turned round to go back
to the house, but the house wasn't there!
Instead there was a *castle*!

10 The children ran around the castle excitedly. Then, they went upstairs. Suddenly Cyril said, 'Oh no! Look at all those soldiers!' 'They're coming to the castle!' said Anthea, 'and they don't look friendly!' 'Why have they got tree trunks?' asked Jane. 'Listen to that noise! They are trying to break the door!' said Robert.

11 'Let's pour water on them,' said Robert. So the children filled pots with water and Robert poured it onto the soldiers. 'Hurry up, sunset!' said Jane.

'Phew!' said Anthea, 'That was dangerous.
Thank goodness in the end everything is OK.'
But Cyril could see something that
Anthea couldn't. 'Oooops!'
he said.

Martha told the children, 'Your mother is coming back today.' The cook said to Martha, 'Did you know a thief took all Lady Grey's beautiful jewels last night?' Jane looked out of the window and said dreamily, 'I wish my mother had beautiful jewels like Lady Grey.' Anthea said, 'Oh no! Don't wish Jane! Quick everyone! Upstairs!'

The children ran upstairs and there, on the bed, were Lady Grey's jewels. 'Oh no!' said Jane, 'What can we do?' Anthea said, 'Let's go and talk to the Sand Fairy.'

▶ 13 The children asked the Sand Fairy for a second wish. 'No!' it said, and began to disappear into the sand. Anthea sat down next to it and said, 'Dear Sand Fairy, please give us a second wish. We promise it's the last wish.' The Sand Fairy stopped digging and said, 'Hmm! What do you want?' Anthea said, 'We don't want the police to find Lady Grey's jewels on our mother's bed! We want Lady Grey to find them in her cupboard.' 'Do you promise this is the last wish?' asked the Sand Fairy. All the children promised quickly. The Sand Fairy got bigger and bigger and bigger and then disappeared into the sand.

14 The children ran back to the house, in through the door, up the stairs and into their mother's bedroom. They looked on the bed but the jewels weren't there. 'Phew!' said Anthea.

Suddenly, Cyril said,
'Come and look.
Here's Mother's car.'
The children looked
out of the window.
Mother was home
again.

1 Write the names. Finish the descriptions.
Draw and colour the faces.

	In the first wish the children had **1** _____ as yellow as the **2** _____ and **3** _____ as blue as the **4** _____	

2 Answer the questions in sentences.

1 Was the Sand Fairy happy?

_____

2 Did it get smaller and smaller?

_____

3 Did the children buy ice creams?

_____

3 Label the picture. You can use the picture dictionary to help you.

1
2
3
4
5
6

4 Circle the correct information. Number the sentences in order.

☐ *Martha / The cook* told *Martha / the cook* about *Mother's / Lady Grey's* jewels.

☐ Jane wished *her mother / she* had *Lady Grey's / Martha's* jewels.

☐ *Martha's / Lady Grey's* jewels were on the bed.

☐ They *gave / didn't give* the Sand Fairy a promise.

☐ The Sand Fairy *didn't give / gave* the *children / Mother* a second wish.

5 Match the rhyming words and write them in the poem.

smile · bit · night · pit · right · while

The Sand Fairy
1 *At the bottom of the garden*
2 *In a big sand _____*
3 *Lived a grumpy Sand Fairy*
4 *Who complained quite a _____!*
5 *It could give you a wish*
6 *And stay for a _____*
7 *But that grumpy Sand Fairy*
8 *It didn't ever _____*
9 *And the wishes that it gave you*
10 *Never worked quite _____*
11 *It was really just as well*
12 *They didn't last till _____!*

6 Match the words in the poem with the definitions.

line 4 *(to) complain*   never

line 4 *quite a bit*   (to) continue

line 8 *didn't ever*   (to) say you're not
                                  happy about
                                  something

line 10 *quite right*   often

line 11 *just as well*   better

line 12 *(to) last*   correctly

7 Imagine you are one of the children. You are telling a friend about the Sand Fairy. Answer the questions to write a conversation.

Friend: Where did you find the Sand Fairy?
Me: _____
_____.

Friend: What was your wish?
Me: _____
_____.

Friend: Did the wish work right?
Me: _____
_____.

Friend: What happened?
Me: _____
_____.

Friend: What happened in the end?
Me: _____
_____.

8 Now work with a partner. Take it in turns to act out your conversations. You can video or record them for the rest of the class.

9 Draw and label the Sand Fairy. Write your wish.

_____

_____

10 Do you like the story? Draw your face.

= I love the story!

= I like the story.

= I quite like the story.

= I don't like the story.